CONNECTING THE DOTS TO INNER PEACE

Why Mindfulness Works and How to Try It

MARK A. MESLER, PH.D.

First published by Dog Ear Publishing
4011 Vincennes Rd
Indianapolis, IN 46268
www.dogearpublishing.net

ISBN: 978-1-4575-4070-7

This book is printed on acid-free paper.

Printed in the United States of America

Contents

ACKNOWLEGEMENTS

Much gratitude to the following friends for their

encouragement and support in the creation of

this little book:

Kathy McBeth,
Roz Grossman,
Mira Bartók
Kristen & Brendan Rush,
Doug & Nan Cooper,
Corey Mesler,
Hannah Eldred,
Jay & Amber Renshaw
and especially Ellie Mesler - my confidante,
companion, and wife of thirty-two years.

We are stardust

We are golden

And we've got to get ourselves

Back to the garden

—Joni Mitchell

•1
Chewing Cud

Did you ever watch a goat chew its cud? I was in my sixties before I did, shortly after my wife started making cheese. Before you know it I was the co-owner of a small goat farm, where I was reminded that goats are members of the ruminant family, like cows and sheep - animals that have four-chambered stomachs and regurgitate a cud for chewing. I know cows are the ones usually depicted as content, but I believe the descriptor extends to the other ruminants as well. When our goats aren't romping around the paddock or engaged in mock combat, they mostly stand in one spot and chew cud - their thin-lipped little mouths working rhythmically, eyes focused softly on the world around them. It's as if the behavior of chewing itself engages an inner calm. It was while observing our goats that I began reflecting on my own efforts at finding such contentment, past and present, and saw the pieces of information I'd accumulated – the dots, so to speak – lining up.

My earliest explorations of inner peace occurred during my late twenties, when I returned to college after the military and two popular books crossed my path: Robert M. Prisig's *Zen and the Art of Motorcycle Maintenance*, and Thaddeus Golas' *The Lazy Man's Guide to Enlightenment*. While Prisig's entertaining story piqued my curiosity enough to try Golas' more specific introduction, I was either too lazy or too distracted by life to pursue this path further at the time, at least deliberately.

The crazy notion that a peace-giving energy exists in us all was introduced to me as a child of the 1960s, when I was informed that we all are made of stardust, and each contain a smidge of the cosmic energy we call God. Now I believe that; it finally makes sense to me, and I have come to understand why mindfulness is a time-tested way of accessing our inherent inner calm.

I also picked up the trail of mindfulness indirectly through the social psychology I studied (symbolic interactionism) during my Ph.D. program, especially in George Herbert Mead's original teachings on the subject, *Mind Self And Society*.

Much like cud-chewing for goats, we humans seem to be blessed with our own built-in access to contentment, and I only recently realized how it relates to Mead's social psychology and our inner voice.

•2

Inner Voice

My introduction to social psychology came as a psychology undergraduate before taking it as the focus of my Ph.D. in sociology. In either discipline, social psychology is basically the study of how an individual's thoughts, feelings and behaviors are influenced by, and in turn influence, the behavior of others. In sociology's version, our internal dialogue, or inner voice, is the key to understanding human behavior. According to Mead, its founding father, it is the development and use of language that allows us not only to communicate with others but with ourselves; our internal dialogue functions to define each situation we encounter and "call out" an appropriate behavior.

Years after my initial immersion in this perspective, I discovered a graphic depiction of its basic principle in a textbook on interpersonal communication. As the diagram suggests, our awareness and attitude - definition of the situation - form the foundation for our behavior. I found this pyramid represention appealing, and used it often as a teacher, but the reality of the relationship depicted is not quite so 'building block' precise. Awareness alone involves a

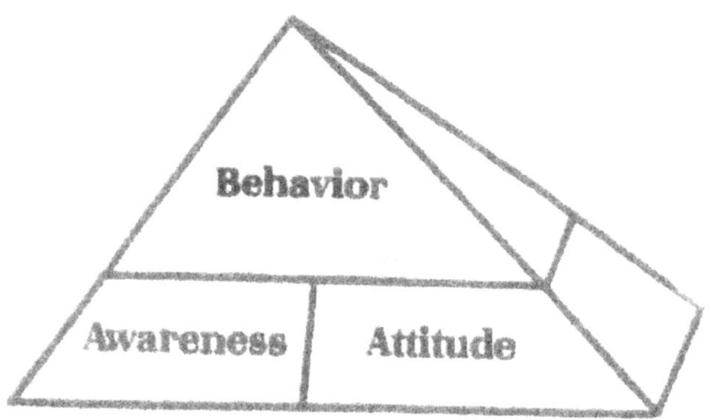

myriad of variables that affect whether and how the situation is perceived, let alone defined and acted upon.

To begin with, we have different levels of consciousness and are aware of many different things at any given time. As a teacher I often used classroom examples to point out this reality. Beyond the first day of choosing a seat, and perhaps adjusting to a new teacher, most of us have attended enough classes in our life that everything else becomes second nature. Classroom days are often spent listening at some level, watching the teacher at times, maybe even taking notes, but all the while your mind is somehow free to wander. And a wandering mind, in case you haven't noticed, is a chatty thing that takes your awareness to many places besides where you are.

Our inner voice is a beautifully adaptive mechanism with a very important function; it guides our behavior in situations ranging from the core brain responses of fight or flight to more nuanced and complex decisions required in everyday life. It also slips readily to other topics when everything around us is status quo. As difficult a task as driving a car was when we first started, and still can be at times, most of us have had the experience, especially when traveling our usual routes, where the routine functions of driving are carried out on a kind of auto pilot. Our awareness and attitude are functioning at some level of consciousness to guide our driving behavior appropriately, but our inner voice is free at a more conscious level to prattle away about oh so many things.

So, the big question is how do we 'quiet' the nagging inner voice to find our own cud-chewing sense of calm? And the answer is alarmingly simple, at least in principle: by shifting our focus from one level of consciousness to another – from the prattling inner voice at one level, to a more serene level that is guided by our inner energy.

•3

Inner Energy

When I first began reading about personal enlightenment back in the 1970s, another popular book came to my attention entitled *Life After Life* - about what I thought at the time was a totally unrelated subject. The author, physician Raymond Moody, had collected more than one hundred personal accounts over the course of five years from people who survived clinical death, or something close to it, and returned to report strikingly similar experiences.

One relatively common experience reported by Moody's subjects was floating above the scene of their surgery, or accident, or other life-threatening incident, looking at the tops of peoples' heads from above and hearing their words as if beside them. Despite the very unusual nature of this experience, they didn't find it the least disconcerting; on the contrary, they reported feelings of extraordinary serenity while separated from their bodies. Some subjects told of their passage through a dark tunnel, and the presence of a brilliant being of light on the other side - a sentient manifestation of love and acceptance, peace and tranquility, in which they became immersed and a part of, where communication occurred without speaking.

Dr. Moody's groundbreaking book seemed to reinforce what many people already believed as part of their cultural heritage – not only that life continues after death, but the manner in which the transition occurs. One of the clearest representations of this heritage is Hieronymous Bosch's late 15th/early 16th century painting, "Ascent Into The Empyrean". Despite being quite intrigued by this information, like my readings on Zen it got tucked away while I continued my formal studies; about a decade passed before I found myself revisiting this subject, within the halls of academe.

After receiving my Ph.D. from the University of Connecticut in 1985, like most new grads I was seeking temporary employment while applying for full-time positions everywhere.

When a local department chair saw that I was a social psychologist with a focus on medicine, he asked if I could substitute-teach a course on Death & Dying, and I said 'Of course.' It was while preparing for that class that I discovered the International Association for Near Death

Studies (IANDS) and a fortuitous coincidence: the Director of IANDS, psychologist Kenneth Ring, was not only one of the foremost researchers on near death experience (NDE), but also a professor at UConn. Like Moody, Dr. Ring had conducted numerous interviews over a five year period with people who reported a NDE and, emboldened by our UConn affiliation, I went looking for his office on campus.

I found it, along with the IANDS headquarters, nestled in the halls of the Psychology Department, where I asked the only person in the office at the time if Dr. Ring might be available. When she said that he was not, I told her about the class I was prepping and asked if he ever offered guest lectures, which I realize in retrospect was naïve given his international following. The woman kindly informed me that while Dr. Ring's schedule could not accommodate me, IANDS would be happy to send a representative to my class, and this turned out better than I ever could have hoped. The same woman showed up with a short documentary film of Dr. Ring's interviews with NDE subjects entitled *Prophetic Voices* – four moving accounts of the emotional impact that NDEs have on otherwise ordinary people.

A heavy equipment operator, for example, describes his encounter with the being of light this way: "You are confronted by true, pure love…In my case, at that moment, I was aware that I could immediately choose to leave and return to reality, or my body. Or, I could have the choice of moving forward, or desiring to enter into, or become part…" tears welled in his eyes and he commented, "rather emotional," before finishing, "…become part of this light." Another subject, a public school superintendent, speaks in similar terms of his experience: "It was a total immersion in light, brightness, warmth, peace, and security…It's difficult to describe; matter of fact it's impossible to describe. Verbally it cannot be expressed. It's something that becomes you, and you become it. I could say I was peace; I was love; I was the brightness. It was part of me."

So powerful is this experience that people often have a difficult time talking about it when they come back. In the film, Ring asks a kindergarten teacher if she remembered her experience at the time of her return, to which she responds, "Yes I did, very vividly, but I did not speak of it for a very long time. Very selectively."   The school superintendent put it this way: "It was at least, at least six months after the incident that I could even speak to my wife about it. It was such an emotional, beautiful swelling feeling inside, that every time I tried to express it, I think I would just explode; you know, I would break down and cry."

After showing the film, the IANDS representative told the class that scientific interest in NDEs had been growing, and physicists were reminding us of two related facts in that regard.

First, all seemingly solid forms, including our bodies, are made up of separate atoms that are connected by energy. Second, one of the few 'laws' of nature is that energy can neither be created nor destroyed; it can only change form. So it makes some sense that our bodies' energy would return to its source: the light at the end of the tunnel.

As compelling as this film and presentation were, for the longest time I struggled to make sense of the information they contained. Even if our inner energy survives physical death, I wondered how it could be that this energy is sentient – capable of thinking, feeling, seeing, hearing, even communicating once separated from our bodies. How is it possible that our inner energy could be the very essence of 'us'? I already know what Ring's subjects would say; in the film he asks a cashier if she was herself while floating above her deathbed, and she responds, "I wasn't myself; I was my mind. I say I was my spirit."

For whatever reason, at that point in my life this just wasn't enough; I still needed something more.

•4
Mind and Spirit

fter that first viewing of *Prophetic Voices* I made a point to get a copy for myself and potential future classes. I've now watched it at least two dozen times, and my response has never wavered; each time I am struck by the earnest truth of these four accounts, themselves representing hundreds more. Nonetheless, my training in Western science instilled in me a healthy enough skepticism that these personal experiences – as numerous and powerful as they were – needed some kind of corroboration. In 1993, after I had been teaching Death and Dying for several years, public television aired a series called *Healing and the Mind*, hosted by Bill Moyers. In that program, I found the confirmation I needed.

The first episode of the series was about *chi*, described as the vital energy force in us all, which provides the foundation for traditional Chinese medicine. Chinese medicine prescribes not only herbs, which are the basis of much Western medication, but also therapies like massage, exercise, and acupuncture to influence the amount and flow of chi through the body. I was only marginally aware of chi at the time, and found this episode a thought-provoking exploration of a very different, Eastern way of perceiving our bodies' energy. It was, however, the next episode in the series – "The Mind Body Connection" - that provided the clearest link to NDEs.

Among the scientific studies highlighted in this segment was one involving neuroscientist David Felton's research on the immune system. Moyers introduces Dr. Felton by asking what it was he discovered through the lens of his microscope that surprised him, and Felton responds, "We saw nerve fibers all over the place, sitting right smack in the middle of some of these cells of the immune system. I looked at it and thought, 'What is this? Everybody says that the nerve fibers are just associated with blood vessels. Why are they out here?'" When Moyers asks him what that means in lay terms Dr. Felton says, "Certainly the thought crossed our minds, 'Geez, I wonder if the nerves might be controlling some of the immune response?' But it was almost, at that time, dogma that the immune system is autonomous, and doesn't have any outside controls. So, we were almost afraid to say anything for fear people would say, 'Geez, don't you know the work of Glutz and his colleagues?' Or they'd come up with some reference that we had never found, and make us look like a bunch of doofuses...."

Dr. Felton goes on to point out that the immune system – the great defense system in the human body – generates its own memory of past insults, and scientists now realize that the immune system's memory communicates in an ongoing way with the other great memory system in the body: the brain. While this was indeed a breakthrough for science, Felton was the first to admit that it was also part of our cultural heritage, reinforcing what our grandmothers had always told us: that what's going on in our thoughts has an effect on the health of our bodies.

In his next interview, Moyers introduces a neuroscientist with a breakthrough that complements Dr. Felton's, and provided the answer I'd been seeking. Here, Dr. Candace Pert explains her discovery of receptors for neuropeptides - what she refers to as the 'molecules of emotion' - where she never expected to find them, on every cell of the human body. This means that every cell communicates with every other about the emotions we're experiencing, so that what we refer to as the 'mind' exists in every cell of our body. That information, in and of it-self, blew my mind – which is to say that every cell of my body was affected by hearing it. And the implication of Dr. Pert's finding goes even further.

Moyers asks at one point in the program if she is saying that the mind 'talks' to the body through these neuropeptides, and she responds with a knowing smile and a question of her own: why is he drawing a distinction between the mind and the body? Moyers answers, as I would have, that it's the way he was taught – the mind is separate from the body. Dr. Pert responds, "Well that just all goes back to a turf deal that Descartes made with the Roman Catholic Church. He got to study science as we know it, and left the soul, and the mind, and consciousness, and emotions in the other realm – that was the realm of the church. Remember, I'm a scientist in the Western tradition, and I don't use the word spirit. I'm not allowed; you know, soul is a four letter word in our tradition."

So if the mind *is* more than the brain, Moyers asks, 'what is the mind?' Pert replies, "The mind? What is the mind? Gosh how frightening. I'm a basic scientist, and I'm having to answer what is the mind." She laughs and, after a moment's thought, says, "The mind is some kind of enlivening energy, that, throughout the brain and body," she indicates the length of her body with a sweep of both hands, "enables the cells to talk to each other."

Here was the corroboration I never expected to get: Western science had actually confirmed that our mind is not confined to the brain; instead, the mind is an "enlivening energy" of thoughts and emotions located in every cell of our body, an energy that is the essence of 'us.' Even Dr. Pert acknowledged that those outside of science might call this energy our spirit; certainly those in the NDE community would.

In 1997 Dr. Pert published a book about the research she discussed with Moyers entitled *Molecules of Emotion*, and ten years later she more directly addressed the connections I'm making here in *Everything You Need to Know to Feel Go(o)d*. Other scientists, too, are beginning to apply their scientific methods to an exploration of the spirit. Cell biologist Bruce Lipton, for example, candidly speaks of the spiritual implications of his work in the 2005 book *The Biology of Belief*, and in accounts like *The Afterlife Experiments* psychologist Gary Schwartz discusses his application of science to the continuation of our spirit beyond corporeal death.

In the wake of these new discoveries, Western culture is slowly adapting its thinking and language to our understanding of body-mind unity, as well as how the mind is to be distinguished from the spirit – the energy that survives death. Whatever conclusion you draw about these matters, the healing potential of the mind - and the healthful effects of mindfulness – finally started making sense to me.

•5

Mindfulness

The concept of mindfulness seems most strongly associated with the tradition of Buddhist meditation, but its practice doesn't have to be either religious or spiritual. If you peruse the literature on the subject you'll see pretty quickly that some teachers of mindfulness are inclined to talk about mind as spirit more than others. Eckhart Tolle, for example, speaks quite directly about mindfulness as spiritual enlightenment, and himself as a spiritual teacher. In his 1997 book *The Power of Now* Tolle describes his approach by saying, "…since every person carries the seed of enlightenment within, I often address myself to the knower in you who dwells behind the thinker, the deeper self that immediately recognizes spiritual truth, resonates with it, and gains strength from it" (p.5).

Jon Kabat-Zinn, on the other hand, is a molecular biologist by training who, while teaching a Buddhist-based meditation, is less inclined to invoke the concept of spirit in his lessons. In his books, *Full Catastrophe Living* and *Wherever You Go There You Are*, he provides straightforward secular lessons in remaining awake to each moment as we experience it. Shortly before his second book was published, he was featured in an episode of Bill Moyers' television series entitled "Healing from Within."

The episode begins with Dr. Kabat-Zinn taking his new pupils, including Moyers, through some meditation exercises, the first of which involves the students accepting a single raisin in the palm of their hands. They are encouraged to examine its size, color and texture, and to feel its weight, before slowly chewing and savoring that simple morsel. As the class continues, the students discover that this focused attention is extended from eating a raisin to the ongoing activity of breathing. They are first provided an introductory lesson on mindful breathing in class, then assigned to repeat that as homework before the next meeting, when they will report their experience with the exercise back to the group. What people most report at their next meeting is an increased awareness of their inner voice, and how it kept distracting them – constantly jumping from one topic to the next. Kabat-Zinn uses this as a teachable moment to say, "This is an important observation, because very often we go through life on a kind of automatic pilot basis. And we kind of aren't even aware that there are all kinds of thoughts going on. They're not subliminal; they're just there, slightly beneath the surface of awareness. But they actually drive many of our actions and behaviors."

Later, during the interview portion of the program, Moyers admits that his mind constantly chatters, to which Kabat-Zinn replies, "This is what meditation is really about, is learning how to recognize that the mind is continually chattering; most people don't even know that. And yet that chatter winds up being the force that drives us much of the day. What meditation is really about is looking deeply into the chatter of the mind, and becoming more aware of its patterns." By observing this inner voice more closely, he explains, you can learn how to relegate it to the back burner, so to speak. You recognize that the inner chatter is there, but consistently come back into the present moment by turning your mind's focus elsewhere, like on your breathing.

Some forms of mindfulness, like transcendental meditation, include a mantra to direct the mind's focus. According to *Webster's Dictionary* a mantra is a "sacred counsel, formula, mystical formula of invocation or incantation (as in Hinduism)." As with mindfulness itself, the use of a mantra to attain it need not be religious or spiritual; I consider it another form of Mead's social psychology – the use of language to define the situation and 'call out' a desired behavior. A mantra, then, is a purposeful use of our inner voice to focus the mind where we choose.

I have a double-barreled mantra: 'Slow down and focus.' It is a simple reminder that helps keep me living in the moment. I wind up saying it to myself on most days at least once, and during stressful times repeatedly. At the end of my career, for example, I was practicing in an outpatient cancer clinic what I once preached in academe, and found myself challenged to maintain the physical pace of organized Western medicine. I remember many days where I kept repeating my relatively new mantra while focusing on the tympanic thermometer I slipped in someone's ear, or the computer keys of my password to access their records, or any number of routine tasks so as to stay wholly present both for myself and the people who might benefit by my being truly there with them.

Then as now, however often I silently speak my mantra, I mean each word quite literally every time. I first remind myself not to rush through the moment, because that is my tendency; I want not only to slow the pace of my body movements, my walking speed for example, but most importantly I want to slow the internal pace at which I'm revving. Also, I find that my slower pace is enhanced when I focus visually on my surroundings, when I literally watch what I'm doing. The point is to be wholly 'present' in each moment. When I am, the result is quite amazing; the time it takes to carry out whatever task I'm involved in doesn't change significantly (by seconds I would guess), yet I immediately feel myself bathed in a quieting sense of calm. By simply tapping the energy of my mind I find peace.

It's worth saying here that my mantra is mine; these words work best for me to align my body-mind. My inner voice still prattles away, but its influence over my being almost disappears because my presence is elsewhere: in the moment. I personally have never set aside a separate time or space for meditating; it seems to be one more thing I'm just too lazy to do. My wife Ellie, however, highly recommends it as a place to start, and return to as needed. I prefer to 'quiet' my inner voice with other means while I'm active, and I found that repeating these four simple words helps to do that, keeping me present in the moment I'm living.

I suggest that you try a mantra yourself. Find a few words that direct your focus to the world around you; call upon your sense of sight, or hearing, taste or smell or touch, or just tell yourself to breathe – be aware of the entrance and exit of your own breath. Take some time right after you finish this chapter to focus on something else – something in the world around you; give it a good minute or so to see what you experience. Maybe you will connect with the peace inside you, maybe not. Maybe your little voice just won't allow that to happen once you've stopped reading. But don't give up; try again later, and even if your first, second or third time is not the charm, not to worry.

Sometimes I'm less able to 'call out' my calmer self, but I now know that an inner peace awaits me when I'm capable of tapping into it.

Sometimes it helps to try different techniques, or combinations - like vision and breathing, or touch and smell - to connect with the serenity that is my mind. And this brings us to our next and final dot.

•6

Sense-Mind Coordination

When I first explored the use of a mantra I didn't call it that; I was just reminding myself what to do – look around at where I am, what I'm doing in the present moment. I'd found that the physical world has sufficient gravity to pull my focus outside, where my inner voice isn't quite so loud. Focusing on my surroundings was a way to keep the prattling on

the back burner while enjoying the present moment.

Because my sense of vision seemed to be
the key to shifting focus, I originally thought
of this process as eye-mind coordination. To
me it seemed very much equivalent to the
hand-eye coordination I was familiar with,
where locking my eyes on a target – whether
shooting hoops, tossing darts, or splitting
wood – gave me a good chance of hitting it.
But since other senses can also be used to attain mindfulness, like the vision, touch, smell
and taste of a single raisin, my original con-
ception needed revision. If any and all senses
can help to focus our mind, I wondered if
what we call hand-eye coordination might be

only one aspect of a larger phenomenon: sense-mind coordination.

When I am capable of being present in the moment, connecting with the peace-giving energy of my mind, the experience very much resembles what athletes refer to as 'being in the zone' – where everything around you seems to slow down, and the object of your sport appears larger than usual. When I was fortunate enough to find myself in the zone playing handball or basketball, my two best sports, opponents seemed a hair slower than I, and the handball or basket seemed a much more accommodating target. In addition, all the while I was playing I felt remarkably focused and calm; my prattling inner voice was virtually nonexistent. In these circumstances, it just may be that our senses have aligned so closely with the energy of our mind that we are capable of playing at a heightened level of consciousness, our whole body fully engaged in the present.

I have no idea how to purposefully attain that zone in sports; perhaps some of the best athletes in their field do (Michael Jordan comes to mind). I do know that athletes often use sense-mind coordination and mindfulness to stay calm and maintain focus. Baseball pitchers can provide fascinating illustrations in this regard – stepping off the mound to spit or clear their nostrils; massaging the ball with both hands – feeling its texture of leather and string;

adjusting their caps, or clothes or shoelaces, all the while taking slow, deep breaths.

For whatever reason, my visual sense seems best suited on a daily basis to ground me in the moment. I do focus my attention on breathing when I go to bed at night, when I'm attempting to idle my engine way down with my eyes closed. Ellie chooses to focus on her breathing during meditation, and sometimes she listens to CDs as well, which employ some combination of soft-spoken words and restful background sounds to direct the mind's focus. Whatever mechanism you chose, and whichever senses you employ to coordinate with your mind, I encourage you to experiment with it.

One of my favorite exercises, one that I return to for the sheer pleasure of it, is taking a minute or two to touch, and examine, rub and smell the bark of a tree. It almost always works to ground me in that moment, which brings me peace. Notice that I said this almost always works, because nothing in my experience is foolproof. In fact, I was walking with my canine companion in a local park one morning, mulling over wordings for this very passage of the book when I decided to take a break and lay my open palm on a particularly gnarly old cedar tree. Its surface was quintessentially coarse and soft at the same time; the scent when I rubbed it was a pungent and earthy delight, and immediately I was engulfed in more words – words for the book, words about what needed doing when I got home, words asking why I was still in my head listening to words. I touched some more, rubbed and smelled more, and ultimately walked away. Ah well.

Nonetheless I stand by that exercise, and highly recommend it. I've noticed that some baseball players seem to engage in a similar exercise while batting; after hitting a sharply grazed foul ball they smell where the ball struck the bat, and often rub their hand across the warm and abraded surface. Maybe there are other motives behind this quirky behavior, wishing for luck perhaps, but it wouldn't surprise me if some are using their senses of smell and touch to stay focused and be present in that moment.

Whatever senses you employ, once your inner voice is no longer the most prominent aspect of your awareness, you will likely find that being wholly present in life is a uniquely positive experience, as well as a healing state. In *Everything You Need to Know to Feel Go(o)d*, Candace Pert refers to the mind's inner peace as our birthright, saying that we are biologically "hard-wired for bliss."

So whether you think of mindfulness as a complex biological mechanism or a little slice of heaven, daily inner peace is available to you, in much the same way that chewing cud seems to bring my goats contentment. It may require more practice on your part than it does the goats to maintain your calmer self, but like most things, the more you do it the easier it becomes. Just as a journey of a thousand miles begins with a single step, each step you take toward mindfulness makes the next one that much easier.

Epilogue

So that was my journey to inner peace, a forty year odyssey of ignoring all the signposts and wending my way there anyway. Mindfulness and living in the moment now make sense to me as awareness of our own mind-body, where an inherent peace is accessible through our physical senses. And the beauty is, there are probably as many ways to reach that aware state as there are snowflakes; I have only scratched the surface of what's out there to learn. Any and all of our physical senses can be called upon in each and every waking moment, pulling our focus from the brain's prattling inner voice to the mind's more peaceful existence – just being, right now, right here.

It is worth noting that I have been privileged in life so far to find comfort in my surroundings; I have clean water to drink, plenty of food, and a safe place to lay my head, which allows me to access the peace inside. There are all too many in this world who are not so fortunate, whose sensory focus on the world around them will not promote ease. I believe that peace still resides within, whatever our circumstances, and that people exist who can help us find it; whose teachings resonate with you and how you find them is a simple matter of exploration.

As you can see, I have taken input and advice from a variety of sources to wind up on this path of mindfulness. For me it is now a daily routine to slow myself down, focus, and enjoy each moment of being and doing as much as possible, whether I'm washing the dishes, mowing the lawn, taking out the garbage, or planning the days ahead. All the while I am quite aware of my chatty inner voice in the background, and the distractions that life brings to bear around me; I am also, however, often able to remain in the calm presence of that peace-giving energy within. For whatever reason, setting time aside for quiet meditation is not something I've tried, yet; while it seems to be the major avenue to mindfulness in practice today, and continues to provide positive results for millions, it isn't the only course available.

So let me leave you with one last something to try in this regard, breathing. I know sight works best for me as a means to daily mindfulness, but breathing really works at so many levels you almost can't go wrong. Think about how many ways you know that breathing is used to coordinate sense and mind, how many of our experiences breathing is used to control. Are you angry? Take a breath. Are you fatigued? Take deep breaths. Want to stop crying? Take several deep breaths. Delivering a baby? You get it. It is why so many mindfulness techniques involve breathing. So if you're looking for a mantra, something to remind yourself to do each day, 'Breathe' isn't a bad one.

Sources

(in order of appearance)

Prisig, Robert M. *Zen and the Art of Motorcycle Maintenance*, New York: William Morrow, 1974.

Golas, Thaddeus *The Lazy Man's Guide to Enlightenment*, Palo Alto: Seed Center, 1972; Layton, Utah: Gibbs Smith, 1995.

Mead, George Herbert *Mind Self And Society*, (C.W. Morris, ed.), Chicago: University of Chicago Press, 1934.

Tindall, William N., Beardsley, Robert S. & Kimberlin, Carole L. *Communication Skills In Pharmacy Practice* (2nd ed.), Philadelphia: Lea & Febiger, 1989.

Moody, Raymond A. Jr. *Life After Life*, New York: Bantam Books/Mockingbird, 1975.

Ring, Kenneth *Life at Death: A Scientific Investigation of the Near Death Experience*, New York: Coward, McCann and Geoghegan, 1980.

Ring, Kenneth *Heading Toward Omega: In Search of the Meaning of the Near Death Experience*, New York: William Morrow, 1984.

Ring, Kenneth "Prophetic Voices" Springfield, MA: Dr. Andrew Silver & WGBY-TV (VHS), 1981.

Moyers, Bill *Healing and the Mind*, New York: Ambrose Video Publishing (DVD), 1993.

Pert, Candace *Molecules of Emotion*, New York: Scribner, 1997.

Pert, Candace *To Feel Go(o)d: The Science and Spirit of Bliss*, Boulder: Sounds True (CD), 2007.

Lipton, Bruce H. *The Biology of Belief: Unleashing the Power of Consciousness, Matter, & Miracles*, Santa Rosa: Mountain of Love/Elite Books, 2005.

Schwartz, Gary & Simon, William L. *The Afterlife Experiments: Breakthrough Scientific Evidence of Life After Death*, New York: Simon & Schuster, 2002.

Tolle, Eckhart *The Power of Now*, Vancouver: Namaste Publishing, 1997.

Kabat-Zinn, Jon *Full Catastrophe Living*, New York: Delacorte Press, 1990.

Kabat-Zinn, Jon *Wherever You Go There You Are*, New York: Hyperion Books, 1994.

Webster's New Collegiate Dictionary, Springfield, MA: G. & C. Merriam Company, 1981.

CPSIA information can be obtained
at www.ICGtesting.com
Printed in the USA
LVOW05s1325091115
461702LV00031B/771/P